To:

_____

From:

_____

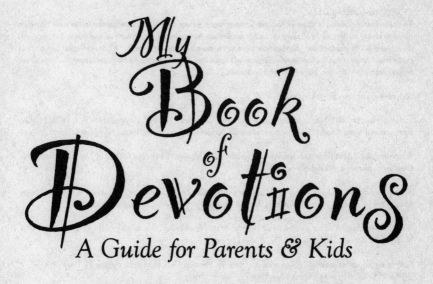

My Book of Devotions

A Guide for Parents & Kids

about Self-control

Simon & Schuster, Inc.

NEW YORK LONDON TORONTO SYDNEY

Simon & Schuster, Inc.
1230 Avenue of the Americas, New York, New York 10020

Scripture quotations are taken from:

Scriptures marked NIV® are from the *Holy Bible, New International Version®*. Copyright © 1973, 1978, 1984 by International Bible Society. Used by permission of Zondervan Publishing House. All rights reserved.

Scriptures marked NKJV are taken from the *New King James Version®*. Copyright © 1982 by Thomas Nelson, Inc. Used by permission. All rights reserved.

Scriptures marked NLT are taken from the *Holy Bible, New Living Translation*. Copyright © 1996. Used by permission of Tyndale House Publishers, Inc., Wheaton, Illinois 60189. All rights reserved.

Scriptures marked NCV are quoted from *The Holy Bible, New Century Version*. Copyright © 1987, 1988, 1991 by Word Publishing, Nashville, TN 37214. Used by permission.

Scripture quotations marked MSG are taken from *The Message*. Copyright © by Eugene H. Peterson 1993, 1994, 1995. Used by permission of NavPress Publishing Group.

Scripture quotations marked ICB are taken from the *International Children's Bible, New Century Version*. Copyright © 1986, 1988 by Word Publishing, Nashville, TN 37214. Used by permission.

Scripture quotations marked Holman CSB are taken from the *Holman Christian Standard Bible®*. Copyright © 1999, 2000, 2002, 2003 by Holman Bible Publishers. Used by permission. Holman Christian Standard Bible®, Holman CSB®, and HCSB® are federally registered trademarks of Holman Bible Publishers.

Cover Design by Kim Russell / Wahoo Designs
Page Layout by Bart Dawson

Manufactured in the United States of America

10 9 8 7 6 5 4 3 2 1

ISBN-13: 978-1-4169-1578-2
ISBN-10: 1-4169-1578-8

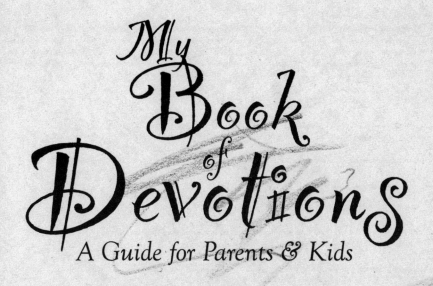

My Book of Devotions

A Guide for Parents & Kids

about Self-control

This is the day that
the LORD has made.
Let us rejoice
and be glad today!

Psalm 118:24 ICB

Table of Contents

A Message to Parents

Perhaps your child's bookshelf is already filled with a happy and helpful assortment of good books for kids. If so, congratulations—that means you're a thoughtful parent who understands the importance of reading to your child. This book is intended to be an important addition to your child's library.

This little text is intended to be read by Christian parents to their young children. The book contains 31 brief chapters, one for each day of the month. Each chapter consists of a Bible verse, a brief story, kid-friendly quotations from notable Christian thinkers, a timely tip, and a prayer. Every chapter examines a different aspect of an important topic: self-control.

For the next 31 days, take the time to read one chapter each night to your child, and then spend a few moments talking about the chapter's meaning. By the end of the month, you will have had 31 different opportunities to share God's wisdom with your son or daughter, and that's good . . . very good.

If you have been touched by God's love and His grace, then you know the joy that He has brought into your own life. Now it's your turn to share His message with the boy or girl whom He has entrusted to your care. Happy reading! And may God richly bless you and yours.

Self-control Means Looking Before You Leap

Trust the Lord with all your heart.
Don't depend on your own understanding.
Remember the Lord in everything you do.
And he will give you success.

Proverbs 3:5-6 ICB

Day 1

Maybe you've heard this old saying: "Look before you leap." What does that saying mean? It means that you should stop and think before you do something. Otherwise, you might be sorry you did it.

Learning how to control yourself is an important part of growing up. The more you learn about self-control, the better. Self-control will help you at home, at school, and at church. That's why parents and teachers are happy to talk about the rewards of good self-control. And that's why you should be excited about learning how important it is to look before you leap . . . not after!

Big Idea for Kids

Think ahead: Before you do something, ask yourself this question: "Will I be ashamed if my parents find out?" If the answer to that question is "Yes," don't do it!

The alternative to discipline is disaster.
Vance Havner

Big Idea for Parents

Wait patiently for your child to grow up. Some bad habits, like impulsive behavior and temper tantrums, are simply a sign of youthful immaturity. If you maintain a steady hand, a loving heart, and a level head, this troubling behavior will, in all likelihood, subside as your child matures.

Today's Prayer

Dear Lord, sometimes I make mistakes.
When I do, forgive me. And help me,
Lord, to learn from my mistakes
so that I can be a better person
and a better example to
my friends and family.
Amen

Listen to
Your Conscience

They show that in their hearts they know
what is right and wrong.

Romans 2:15 ICB

Day 2

God gave you something called a conscience: some people describe it as a little voice, but really, it's a feeling—it's a feeling that tells you whether something is right or wrong. Your conscience will usually tell you what to do and when to do it. Pay attention to that feeling, and trust it.

If you slow down and listen to your conscience, you'll usually stay out of trouble. And if you listen to your conscience, it won't be so hard to control your own behavior. Why? Because most of the time, your conscience already knows right from wrong. So don't be in such a hurry to do things. Instead of "jumping right in," listen to your conscience. In the end, you'll be very glad you did.

Big Idea for Kids

If you're not sure what to do . . . trust your conscience. It's almost always right!

A quiet conscience sleeps in thunder.
Thomas Fuller

Big Idea for Parents

Where should they learn right from wrong? When it comes to teaching Christian values to our children, home school is always in session. Preach, teach, and behave accordingly.

Today's Prayer

Dear Lord, You have given me
a conscience that tells me what is
right and what is wrong. I will listen
to that quiet voice so I can do
the right thing today and every day.
Amen

Patience Please!

Always be humble and gentle.
Be patient and accept each other with love.
Ephesians 4:2 ICB

Day 3

Do you want to learn self-control? Then you must learn the art of being patient. The dictionary defines the word "patience" as "the ability to be calm, tolerant, and understanding." Here's what that means: the word "calm" means being in control of your emotions (not letting your emotions control you). The word "tolerant" means being kind and considerate to people who are different from you. And, the word "understanding" means being able to put yourself in another person's shoes.

If you can be calm, tolerant, and understanding, you will be the kind of person whose good deeds are a blessing to your family and friends. And that's exactly the kind of person that God wants you to be.

Big Idea for Kids

What's good for you is good for them, too: If you want others to be patient with you, then you should treat them in the same way. That's the Golden Rule, and it should be your rule, too!

> Patience achieves more than force.
> Edmund Burke

Big Idea for Parents

They learn by watching: Kids imitate their parents, so act accordingly! The best way for your child to learn to be patient is by example . . . your example!

Today's Prayer

Lord, sometimes I am not very patient.
Slow me down and calm me down.
Help me to think wisely and to
act wisely. Today and every day,
help me to learn the wisdom
of patience.
Amen

Following Directions

In all your ways acknowledge Him,
and He shall direct your paths.

Proverbs 3:6 NKJV

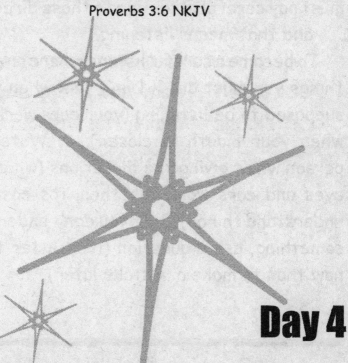

Day 4

Directions, directions, directions. It seems like somebody is always giving you directions: telling you where to go, how to behave, and what to do next. But sometimes all these directions can be confusing! How can you understand everything that everybody tells you? The answer, of course, is that you must pay careful attention to those directions . . . and that means listening.

To become a careful listener, here are some things you must do: 1. Don't talk when you're supposed to be listening (your ears work best when your mouth is closed); 2. Watch the person who's giving the directions (when your eyes and ears work together, it's easier to understand things); 3. If you don't understand something, ask a question (it's better to ask now than to make a mistake later).

Big Idea for Kids

If you're afraid to raise your hand and ask a question, remember this . . . if you don't understand something, lots of other people in the classroom probably don't understand it either. So you'll be doing everybody a big favor if you raise your hand and

> Obedience is the outward expression
> of your love of God.
> Henry Blackaby

Big Idea for Parents

Giving directions? Here are a few tips: Be friendly; speak slowly; encourage lots of questions; give lots of examples; say it in several different ways; use repetition.

Today's Prayer

Dear Lord, let me listen carefully
to my parents, to my teachers,
and to You. When I listen, I learn.
Let me become a better listener
today than I was yesterday,
and let me become an even better
listener tomorrow.
Amen

Knowing Right from Wrong . . . and Doing It!

Praise the Lord! Happy are those
who respect the Lord,
who want what he commands.

Psalm 112:1 NCV

Day 5

If you're old enough to know right from wrong, then you're old enough to do something about it. In other words, you should always try to do the right thing, and you should also do your very best not to do the wrong thing.

The more self-control you have, the easier it is to do the right thing. Why? Because when you learn to think first and do things next, you avoid lots of silly mistakes. So here's great advice: first, slow down long enough to figure out the right thing to do—and then do it. You'll make yourself happy, and you'll make lots of other people happy, too.

Big Idea for Kids

When in doubt, ask mom or dad: If you're not sure whether or not something is right or wrong, ask your parents before you do it!

> Obedience to God is our job.
> Elisabeth Elliot

Big Idea for Parents

Listen with your ears, your eyes, and your heart. And remember: wise parents pay careful attention to the things their children don't say.

Today's Prayer

Dear Lord, when I'm tempted to do
the wrong thing, help me to slow down
and to think about my behavior.
And then, help me to know what's right
and to do what's right.
Amen

Parents Can Help

Honor your father and your mother.
Exodus 20:12 ICB

Day 6

Whenever you want to get better at something, you should always be willing to let your parents help out in any way they can. After all, your parents want you to become the very best person you can be. So, if you want to become better at controlling your own behavior, ask your parents to help. How can they help out? By reminding you to slow down and think about things before you do them—not after. It's as simple as that.

Big Idea for Kids

Calm down . . . sooner rather than later! If you're angry with a friend or family member, don't blurt out something unkind. If you can't say anything nice, go to your room and don't come out until you can.

Examine yourselves—ask, each of you,
"Have I been a good brother? . . . son? . . .
husband? . . . father? . . . servant?"
Charles Kingsley

Big Idea for Parents

Hey Mom and Dad, how do you treat your parents? If you're lucky enough to have parents who are living, remember that the way you treat them is the way you're training your kids to treat you.

Today's Prayer

Dear Lord, You have given me a family
that cares for me and loves me.
Thank You. Let me love everybody
in my family, even when they're
not perfect. And let me always be
thankful that my family loves me,
even when I'm not perfect.
Amen

Slowing Down Long Enough to Listen

Wise people can also listen and learn.
Proverbs 1:5 NCV

Day 7

When God made you, he gave you two ears and one mouth for a very good reason: you can learn at least twice as much by listening as you can by talking. That's why it's usually better to listen first and talk second. But when you're frustrated or tired, it's easy to speak first and think later.

A big part of growing up is learning how to slow down long enough to listen to the things that people have to say. So the next time you're tempted to turn off your ears and tune up your mouth, stop, listen, and think. After all, God gave you two wonderful ears for a very good reason: to use them.

Big Idea for Kids

Listening Shows You Care: When you listen to the things other people have to say, it shows that you care about their message and about them. Listening carefully is not just the courteous thing to do; it's also the kind thing to do.

> People don't care how much you know
> until they know how much you care.
> Zig Ziglar

Big Idea for Parents

Listen first, then speak: For most parents, the temptation to lecture is great; it takes conscious effort to hold one's tongue until one's ears are fully engaged. When a parent is able to do so, his or her efforts are usually rewarded.

Today's Prayer

Dear Lord, I have lots to learn.
Help me to watch, to listen, to think,
and to learn, every day of my life.
Amen

When the Teacher Isn't Looking

The honest person will live safely,
but the one who is dishonest will be caught.
Proverbs 10:9 ICB

Day 8

When your teachers or parents aren't watching, what should you do? The answer, of course, is that you should behave exactly like you would if they were watching you. But sometimes you may be tempted to do otherwise.

When a parent steps away or a teacher looks away, you may be tempted to say something or do something that you would not do if they were standing right beside you. But remember this: when nobody's watching, it's up to you to control yourself. And that's exactly everybody wants you to do: your teachers want you to control yourself, and so do your parents. And so, by the way, does God.

Big Idea for Kids

Behavior you can be proud of: When teachers or parents aren't looking, it's up to you to control yourself. So think about what you're doing, and think about the consequences of your behavior.

Character is what you are in the dark.

D. L. Moody

Big Idea for Parents

Self-control at school starts at home: teachers can certainly help, but we cannot expect them to re-train our children. When it comes to the importance of self-control, we, as parents, must be the ones to teach our kids how to behave.

Today's Prayer

Dear Lord, sometimes it's easier to misbehave than it is to slow down and think about the best way to behave. But even when doing the right thing is difficult, let me slow down long enough to think about the right thing to say or do.

Amen

The Rewards of Self-control

So prepare your minds for service
and have self-control.
1 Peter 1:13 NCV

Day 9

Who needs to learn more about self-control? You do! Why? Well, for one thing, you'll discover that good things happen to people (like you) who are wise enough to think ahead and smart enough to look before they leap.

Whether you're at home or at school, you'll learn that the best rewards go to the kids who control their behavior—not to the people who let their behaviors control them!

Big Idea for Kids

Use the Golden Rule to help you decide what to say and how to behave: Treat people like you want to be treated!

Nobody is good by accident.
No person ever became holy by chance.
C. H. Spurgeon

Big Idea for Parents

Be Disciplined in Your Own Approach to Life: You can't teach it if you won't live it.

Today's Prayer

Dear Lord, You have given me so many blessings, and You want to give me even more. Thank You. Here's how I will show my thanks: I will use my talents, and I will behave myself.

Amen

Stop, Look, and Think!

A wise person is patient.
Proverbs 19:11 ICB

Day 10

The Book of Proverbs tells is that self-control and patience are very good things to have. But for most of us, self-control and patience can also be very hard things to learn.

Are you having trouble being patient? And are you having trouble slowing down long enough to think before you act? If so, remember that self-control takes practice, and lots of it, so keep trying. And if you make a mistake, don't be too upset. After all, if you're going to be a really patient person, you shouldn't just be patient with others; you should also be patient with yourself.

Big Idea for Kids

Stop, think, then speak: If you want to make your words useful instead of hurtful, don't open your mouth until you've turned on your brain!

Teach us, O Lord, the discipline of patience,
for to wait is often harder
than to work.
Peter Marshall

Big Idea for Parents

Words, words, words . . . are important, important, important! And, some of the most important words you will ever speak are the ones that your children hear. So whether or not you are. talking directly to your kids, choose your words carefully.

Today's Prayer

Dear Lord, let me be patient with other people's mistakes. And let me be patient with my own. I know that I still have so many things to learn. I won't stop learning, I won't give up, and I won't stop growing up. Every day, I will do my best to become a more patient person with your help.

Amen

Learning Lessons from Our Mistakes...
the First Time

A wise person pays attention
to correction that will improve his life.
Proverbs 15:31 ICB

Do you ever make mistakes? Of course you do . . . everybody does. And when you make a mistake, it's not so terrible if you learn something. Why should you try to learn from your mistakes? So you won't make the very same mistakes again.

When you have done things that you regret, you should apologize, you should clean up the mess you've made, you should learn from your mistakes, and—last but not least—you should forgive yourself. Mistakes happen . . . it's simply a fact of life, and it's simply a part of growing up. So don't be too hard on yourself, especially if you've learned something along the way.

Big Idea for Kids

Made a mistake? Ask for forgiveness. If you've broken one of God's rules, you can always ask Him for His forgiveness. And He will always give it!

God is able to take mistakes, when they are committed to Him, and make of them something for our good and for His glory.

Ruth Bell Graham

Big Idea for Parents

When angels fall . . . Even your own angelic child may make a mistake on occasion. When the unlikely happens, help your boy or girl understand why the behavior is wrong and how to prevent it in the future.

Today's Prayer

Dear Lord, sometimes I make mistakes.
When I do, help me learn something,
help me forgive myself, and help me
become a smarter person today
than I was yesterday.
Amen

The Golden Rule

This royal law is found in the Scriptures:
"Love your neighbor as yourself."
If you obey this law,
then you are doing right.
James 2:8 ICB

Day 12

When we learn how to control ourselves, we can be more considerate of other people. Would you like to make the world a better place? If so, you can start by practicing the Golden Rule.

Jesus said, "Do to others what you want them to do to you" (Mathew 7:12 NCV). That means that that you should treat other people in the very same way that you want to be treated. That's the Golden Rule.

Jesus wants us to treat other people with respect, kindness, courtesy, and love. When we do, we make our families and friends happy . . . and we make our Father in heaven very proud. So if you want to know how to treat other people, ask the person you see every time you look into the mirror. The answer you receive will tell you exactly what to do.

Big Idea for Kids

How would you feel? When you're trying to decide how to treat another person, ask yourself this question: "How would I feel if somebody treated me that way?" Then, treat the other person the way that you would want to be treated.

> The Golden Rule starts at home,
> but it should never stop there.
>
> Marie T. Freeman

Big Idea for Parents

Words are never enough: When it comes to teaching our children the most important lessons, the things we say pale in comparison to the things we do. Being a responsible parent is a big job, but don't fret: you and God, working together, can handle it!

Today's Prayer

Dear Lord, help me always to do
my very best to treat others as
I wish to be treated.
The Golden Rule is Your rule, Father;
let me also make it mine.
Amen

What the Bible Says

Your word is like a lamp for my feet
and a light for my way.
Psalm 119:105 ICB

Day 13

What book contains everything that God has to say about self-control? The Bible, of course. If you read the Bible every day, you'll soon be convinced that self-control is very important to God. And, since doing the right thing (and the smart thing) is important to your Father in heaven, it should be important to you, too.

The Bible is the most important book you'll ever own. It's God's Holy Word. Read it every day, and follow its instructions. When you do, you'll be safe now and forever.

Big Idea for Kids

Read the Bible? Every Day! Try to read your Bible with your parents every day. If they forget, remind them!

> The Bible is God's Word, given to us by God Himself so we can know Him and His will for our lives.
>
> Billy Graham

Big Idea for Parents

It's up to us: Our children will learn about Jesus at church and, in some cases, at school. But, the ultimate responsibility for religious teachings should never be delegated to institutions outside the home. As parents, we must teach our children about the love and grace of Jesus Christ by our words and by our actions.

Today's Prayer

Dear Lord, the Bible is Your gift to me.
Let me use it, let me trust it,
and let me obey it, today
and every day that I live.
Amen

Homewerk

Remember what you are taught.
And listen carefully to words of knowledge.
Proverbs 23:12 ICB

Day 14

Sooner or later, you'll start getting homework, and when that day comes, you'd better be ready because that's when you'll really need lots of self-control! Usually, homework isn't hard to do, but it takes time. And sometimes we'd rather be doing other things (like playing outside or watching TV). But, when we put off our homework until the last possible minute, we make it hard on ourselves.

Instead of putting off your homework, do it first. Then, you'll have the rest of your time to have fun—and you won't have to worry about all that homework.

Big Idea for Kids

The habit of putting things off . . . is a habit that you're better off without.

Not now becomes never.
Martin Luther

Big Idea for Parents

Teach by Example: Whatever "it" is, do it now. When you do, you'll demonstrate to your child the value of self-discipline.

Today's Prayer

Dear Lord, You have given me
a wonderful gift: time here on earth.
Let me use it wisely today
and every day that I live.
Amen

Quiet Please

In quietness and confidence
shall be your strength.
Isaiah 30:15 NKJV

Day 15

Have you learned how to sit quietly and listen to your parents and your teachers? Have you learned how to listen respectfully—with your ears open wide and your mouth closed tight? If so, give yourself a big pat on the back (or if you can't reach way back there, ask your mom or dad to do it for you!).

An important part of learning self-control is learning how to be quiet when you're supposed to be quiet. It isn't always easy, but the sooner you learn how to sit quietly and behave respectfully, the better. So you might as well start today.

Big Idea for Kids

And when you speak, be respectful to everybody, starting with parents, grandparents, teachers, and adults . . . but don't stop there. Be respectful of everybody, including yourself!

A quiet time is a basic ingredient
in a maturing relationship with God.
Charles Stanley

Big Idea for Parents

Silence is Okay: Sometimes, just being there is enough. If you're not sure what to say, it's okay to say nothing.

Today's Prayer

Dear Lord, let me listen respectfully
to my parents, to my teachers,
and to You. I have much to learn.
Let me learn as much as I can as soon
as I can, and let me be a good example
for other people to follow.
Amen

Parents Are Smarter Than You Think

My child, listen to your father's teaching.
And do not forget your mother's advice.

Proverbs 1:8 ICB

Day 16

Do you listen carefully to the things your parents tell you? You should. Your parents want the very best for you. They want you to be happy and healthy; they want you to be smart and to do smart things. Your parents have much to teach you, and you have much to learn. So listen carefully to the things your mom and dad have to say. And ask lots of questions. When you do, you'll soon discover that your parents have lots of answers . . . lots of very good answers.

Big Idea for Kids

Talking versus Really Talking: Don't be too embarrassed or too fearful to tell your parents what you're really thinking about. They understand more than you think they do!

The home should be a school where
life's basic lessons are taught.
Billy Graham

Big Idea for Parents

Some choices WE must make: of course, we want to give our children room to grow, but some decisions must be reserved for the wisest men and women of the family (us). Those choices include matters of personal health and safety and the core principles by which we, as parents, intend to raise our families.

Today's Prayer

Lord, let me be respectful of all people, starting with my family and friends. And, let me share the love that I feel in my heart with them . . . and with You!
Amen

No More Tantrums

Do not become angry easily.
Anger will not help you live
a good life as God wants.
James 1:19 ICB

Day 17

Temper tantrums are one of the silliest ways to lose self-control. Why? Because when we lose our temper, we say things that we shouldn't say, and we do things that we shouldn't do. And to make matters worse, once the tantrum is over, we usually feel embarrassed or worse. Too bad!

The Bible tells us that it is usually foolish to become angry and that it is wise to remain calm. That's why we should learn to control our tempers before our tempers control us.

Big Idea for Kids

Think carefully . . . make that very carefully!
If you're a little angry, think carefully before
you speak. If you're very angry, think very
carefully. Otherwise, you might say something
mean that you'll be sorry you said.

When you strike out in anger,
you may miss the other person,
but you will always hit yourself.
Jim Gallery

Big Idea for Parents

Keeping Your Cool 101: When your child
becomes upset, you'll be tempted to become
upset, too. Resist that temptation. Remember
that in a house full of kids and grown-ups,
you're the grown-up. And it's up to you to
remain calm even when other, less mature
members of the family can't.

Today's Prayer

Dear Lord, help me to turn away from
angry thoughts and angry people.
Help me always to use Jesus as
my guide for life, and let me trust
His promises today and forever.
Amen

Being an Example to Others

You are the light that gives light to
the world. In the same way, you should be
a light for other people. Live so that they
will see the good things you do and
will praise your Father in heaven.

Matthew 5:14,16 NCV

Day 18

What kind of example are you? Are you the kind of person who shows other people what it means to be well-behaved? And, are you learning to use more and more self-control? Hopefully so!!!

Whether you realize it or not, you're an example to your friends and family members. So today, be a good example for others to follow. Because God needs people (like you) who are willing to behave themselves as God intends. And that's exactly the kind of example you should try to be.

Big Idea for Kids

Look around! Someone very near you may need a helping hand or a kind word, so keep your eyes open, and look for people who need your help, whether at home, at church, or at school.

Living life with a consistent spiritual walk deeply influences those we love most.

Vonette Bright

Big Idea for Parents

Teaching Values: Your children will learn about life from many sources; the most important source can and should be you. But remember that the lectures you give are never as important as the ones you live. So teach the importance of self-control every day and, if necessary, use words.

Today's Prayer

Lord, make me a worthy example to my family and friends. And, let my words and my deeds serve as a testimony to the changes You have made in my life. Let me praise You, Father, by following in the footsteps of Your Son, and let others see Him through me.

Amen

Listen . . . and Obey

Teach me, O Lord, the way of Your statutes,
and I shall keep it to the end.
Give me understanding, and I shall keep
Your law; indeed, I shall observe it
with my whole heart.

Psalm 119:33-34 NKJV

Day 19

When you learn to control your actions and your words, you will find it easier to obey your parents, your teachers, and your Father in heaven. Why? Because in order to be an obedient person, you must first learn how to control yourself—otherwise, you won't be able to obey very well, even when you want to.

When you learn the importance of obedience, you'll soon discover that good things happen when you behave yourself. And the sooner you learn to listen and obey, the sooner those good things will start happening.

Big Idea for Kids

Obeying God? Yes! What about the rules you learn about in the Bible? Well, those aren't just any old rules—they're God's rules. And you should behave—and obey—accordingly.

God will never reveal more truth
about Himself until you have obeyed
what you know already.

Oswald Chambers

Big Idea for Parents

See as much as you can; correct as much as you should: Teaching your child the important of disciplined behavior requires an observing eye and a patient heart. You should expect your child to be well-behaved, but you should not expect your child to be perfect. In fact, an important part of parenting is knowing what to overlook and when to overlook it.

Today's Prayer

Dear Lord, You know what's best
for me. I will study Your Word
and obey Your teachings
this day and forever.
Amen

You Don't Have to Go Along with the Crowd

Do you think I am trying to make people accept me? No, God is the One I am trying to please. Am I trying to please people? If I still wanted to please people, I would not be a servant of Christ.

Galatians 1:10 NCV

Day 20

It happens to all of us at one time or another: a friend asks us to do something that we think is wrong. What should we do? Should we try to please our friend by doing something bad? No way! It's not worth it!

Trying to please our friends is okay. What's not okay is misbehaving in order to do so.

Do you have a friend who encourages you to misbehave? Hopefully you don't have any friends like that. But if you do, say "No, NO, NOOOO!" And what if your friend threatens to break up the friendship? Let him! Friendships like that just aren't worth it.

Big Idea for Kids

Face facts: since you can't please everybody, you're better off trying to please the people who are trying to help you become a better person, not the people who are encouraging you to misbehave!

Those who follow the crowd
usually get lost in it.
Rick Warren

Big Idea for Parents

Remind your child . . . that it's more important to be respected than to be liked.

Today's Prayer

Dear Lord, there's a right way
and a wrong way to do things.
Let me do what's right and keep doing
what's right every day of my life.
Amen

If You're Not Sure What to Do

I will instruct you and teach you
in the way you should go;
I will guide you with My eye.

Psalm 32:8 NKJV

Day 21

When you're not sure whether something is right or wrong, ask yourself a simple question: "How would Jesus behave if He were here?" The answer to that question will tell you what to do.

Jesus was perfect, but we are not. Still, we must try as hard as we can to do the best that we can. When we do, we will love others, just as Christ loves us.

Big Idea for Kids

When in doubt: do the thing that you think Jesus would do. And, of course, don't do something if you think that He wouldn't do it.

God's Word is a light not only to
our path but also to our thinking.
Place it in your heart today,
and you will never walk in darkness.
Joni Eareckson Tada

Big Idea for Parents

Want them to know what Jesus would do? Then teach them what Jesus did!

Today's Prayer

Dear Lord, even when I don't
understand why things happen,
I will trust You. Even when I am
confused or worried, I will trust You.
There are many things that
I cannot do, Lord, and there are
many things that I cannot understand.
But one thing I can do is trust in You.
Amen

Learning to Wait Your Turn

Patience is better than strength.

Proverbs 16:32 ICB

Day 22

When we're standing in line or waiting our turn, it's tempting to push ahead of other people. And it's tempting to scream, "Me first!", but it's the wrong thing to do! The Bible tells us that we shouldn't push ahead of others; instead, we should do the right thing—and the polite thing—by saying, "You first!"

Sometimes, waiting your turn can be hard, especially if you're excited or in a hurry. But even then, waiting patiently is the right thing to do. Why? Because parents say so, teachers say so, and, most importantly, God says so!

Big Idea for Kids

God and your parents have been patient with you . . . now it's your turn to be patient with others.

Patience is the companion of wisdom.
St. Augustine

Big Idea for Parents

Be patient with your child's impatience: children are supposed to be more impulsive than adults; after all, they're still kids. So be understanding of your child's limitations and understanding of his or her imperfections.

Today's Prayer

Lord, sometimes it's hard to be
a patient person, and that's exactly
when I should try my hardest
to be patient. Help me to be patient
and kind, even when it's hard.
Amen

Safety First

Innocent people will be kept safe.
But those who are dishonest
will suddenly be ruined.
Proverbs 28:18 ICB

Day 23

Self-control and safety go hand in hand. Why? Because a big part of self-control is looking around and thinking things through before you do something that you might regret later.

Remember the saying "Look before you leap!"? Well, if you want to live safely and happily, you should look very carefully before you decide whether or not to leap. After all, it's easy to leap, but once you're in the middle of your jump, it's too late to leap back!

Big Idea for Kids

Don't complain about safety: whether it's a fire drill at school or wearing seat belts in the family car, don't whine, complain, or resist. When grown-ups are trying to keep you safe, your job is to help them do it!

The Will of God will never take you where the Grace of God will not protect you.

Anonymous

Big Idea for Parents

Thinking ahead for your child: As a responsible parent, it's up to you to be your family's safety expert. Impulsive kids, left to their own devices, tend to get themselves into dangerous situations; responsible adults, however, don't leave kids to their own devices.

Today's Prayer

Dear Lord, You protect me; help me
to learn how to protect myself.
Help me to slow down, to think ahead,
and to look before I leap. You are
concerned with my safety, Lord.
Help me to be concerned with it, too.
Amen

When In Doubt, Slow Down

Be still, and know that I am God.
Psalm 46:10 NKJV

Day 24

Maybe you're one of those people who try to do everything fast, faster, or fastest! If so, maybe you sometimes do things before you think about the consequences of your actions. If that's the case, it's probably a good idea to slow down a little bit so you can think before you act. When you do, you'll soon discover the value of thinking carefully about things before you get started. And while you're at it, it's probably a good idea to think before you speak, too. After all, you'll never have to apologize for something that you didn't say.

Big Idea for Kids

Got Questions? If you're faced with too many questions and too few answers, slow down, and talk to your parents. When you do, you'll discover that your patents probably have more answers than you have questions.

> You can always go to God with
> your questions. You may not find all
> the answers, but in finding God,
> you know the One who does.
>
> Max Lucado

Big Idea for Parents

Put the brakes on impulsive behavior . . . theirs and yours!

Today's Prayer

Dear Lord, sometimes this world can be a puzzling place. When I am unsure what to do, let me be quick to learn from my parents, and let me be quick to learn from You.

Amen

What It Means to Be Wise

Wisdom begins with respect for the Lord.
Proverbs 9:10 ICB

Day 25

If you look in a dictionary, you'll see that the word "wisdom" means "using good judgement, and knowing what is true." But there's more: it's not just enough to know what's right; if you really want to become a wise person, you must also do what's right.

A big part of "doing what's right" is learning self-control . . . and the best day to start learning self-control is this one!

Big Idea for Kids

Learning about Jesus: Start learning about Jesus, and keep learning about Him as long as you live. His story never grows old, and His teachings never fail.

> Wisdom always waits for the right time
> to act, while emotion always pushes
> for action right now.
> Joyce Meyer

Big Idea for Parents

Stress the Importance of Learning: Some families stress the importance of education more than other families. Make yours a home in which the importance of education is clearly a high priority.

Today's Prayer

Dear Lord, I trust Your wisdom.
The most important wisdom is Yours,
and the most important truth is Yours.
Today, I will show my respect for
You by obeying your commandments.
Amen

Don't Give Up

We must not become tired of doing good.
Galatians 6:2 ICB

Day 26

If you're having trouble learning how to control your actions or your emotions, you're not alone! Most people have problems with self-control from time to time, so don't be discouraged. Just remember that self-control requires practice and lots of it. So if you're a little discouraged, don't give up. Just keep working on improving your self-control until you get better at it. . . . and if you keep trying, you can be sure that sooner or later, you will get better at it.

Big Idea for Kids

Everybody is a VIP: VIP means "Very Important Person." To God, everybody is a VIP, and we should treat every person with dignity, patience, and respect

Keep adding, keep walking, keep advancing;
do not stop, do not turn back,
do not turn from the straight road.

St. Augustine

Big Idea for Parents

Self-control is as self-control does: Your children will learn about self-control by watching you (not by listening to you!). It's a scary thought, of course, but with God's help, you're up to the task!

Today's Prayer

Dear Lord, help me to make
Your world a better place. I can't fix
all the world's troubles, but I can help
make things better with kind words,
good deeds, and sincere prayers.
Let my actions and my prayers be
pleasing to You, Lord, now and forever.
Amen

Pray About It

Always be happy. Never stop praying.
Give thanks whatever happens.
That is what God wants for you
in Christ Jesus.
1 Thessalonians: 5:16-18 ICB

Day 27

Do you really want to become a more patient person? Then pray about it. Would you like to learn how to use better self-control? Then pray about it. If you are upset, pray about it. If there is something you're worried about, ask God to comfort you. And as you pray more, you'll discover that God is always near and that He's always ready to hear from you. So don't worry about things; pray about them. God is waiting . . . and listening!

Big Idea for Kids

Pray early and often: One way to make sure that your heart is in tune with God is to pray often. The more you talk to God, the more He will talk to you.

I have found the perfect antidote for fear.
Whenever it sticks up its ugly face,
I clobber it with prayer.

Dale Evans Rogers

Big Idea for Parents

Be a prayerful parent: God is listening, and your children are watching.

Today's Prayer

Dear Lord, help me remember
the importance of prayer.
You always hear my prayers, God;
let me always pray them!
Amen

You'll Be Happier

Happy is the person who . . .
loves what the Lord commands.

Psalm 112:1 ICB

Day 28

Do you want to be happy? Here are some things you should do: Love God and His Son, Jesus; obey the Golden Rule; learn how to control yourself, and always try to do what you think is right. When you do these things, you'll discover that happiness goes hand-in-hand with good behavior.

The happiest people do not misbehave; the happiest people are not cruel or thoughtless. The happiest people don't say unkind things. The happiest people are those who love God and follow His rules—starting, of course, with the Golden one.

Big Idea for Kids

Better self-control can help make you happy: the better you behave, the more fun you'll have. And don't let anybody try to tell you otherwise.

Christ is the secret, the source,
the substance, and the center of
all true and lasting gladness.
Mrs. Charles E. Cowman

Big Idea for Parents

Parents make the best encouragers! You're not just your children's parents; you're also their biggest fans. Make sure they know it.

Today's Prayer

Dear Lord, I am thankful for all
the blessings You have given me.
Let me be a happy Christian, Father,
as I share Your joy with friends,
with family, and with the world.

Amen

When Nobody Is Around

Good people will be guided by honesty;
dishonesty will destroy those who
are not trustworthy.
Proverbs 11:3 NCV

Day 29

Even when nobody's watching, God is. And He knows whether you've done the right thing or the wrong thing. So if you're tempted to misbehave when nobody is looking, remember this: There is never a time when "nobody's watching." Somebody is always watching over you—and that Somebody, of course, is your Father in Heaven. Don't let Him down!

Big Idea for Kids

Want something? Ask, don't take! It's okay to ask. It's not okay to take!

Integrity is a sign of maturity.
Charles Swindoll

Big Idea for Parents

Displaying integrity in matters both great and small: Right is right and wrong is wrong whether the issue appears large or inconsequential. And when it comes to issues of integrity, you are a 24-hour-a-day example to your child, so be on guard.

Today's Prayer

Dear Lord, help me to behave myself
like a good Christian! Let me keep
Christ in my heart, and let me put
the devil in his place:
far away from me!
Amen

Because It's What God Wants

"Not My will, but Yours, be done."
Luke 22:42 NKJV

Day 30

How much does God love you? He loves you so much that He sent His Son Jesus to come to this earth for you! And, when you accept Jesus into your heart, God gives you a gift that is more precious than gold: that gift is called "eternal life," which means that you will live forever with God in heaven!

God's love is bigger and more powerful than anybody can imagine, but it is very real. So do yourself a favor right now: accept God's love with open arms and welcome His Son Jesus into your heart. When you do, your life will be changed today, tomorrow, and forever.

Big Idea for Kids

Self-control every day: Self-control should be part of our lives every day, not just on the days when we feel good. God loves us every day and we should obey Him every day. And remember: good behavior starts with you, but if you're a good example to others, it won't end there!

> Life in God is a great big hug
> that lasts forever!
> Barbara Johnson

Big Idea for Parents

He's watching us, too. Of course, we know that God watches over us, but we must also make certain that our children know that we know. And, we must behave in ways that let our children know that we know that He knows. Whew!

Today's Prayer

Dear Lord, thank You for watching
over me. Help me understand
what's right and do what's right,
today and always.
Amen

Your Friend Forever

And Jesus said to them,
"I am the bread of life. He who comes to Me
shall never hunger, and he who believes in
Me shall never thirst."
John 6:35 NKJV

Day 31

There's an old song that says, "What a friend we have in Jesus." Those words are certainly true! When you invite Him into your heart, Jesus will be your friend forever. If you make mistakes, He'll still be your friend. If you behave badly, He'll still love you. If you feel sorry or sad, He can help you feel better if you ask Him to.

Jesus wants you to have a happy, healthy life. He wants you to behave yourself, and He wants you to take care of yourself. And now, it's up to you to do your best to live up to the hopes and dreams of your very best friend: Jesus.

Big Idea for Kids

Jesus loves me, this I know . . . but how much? Here's how much: Jesus loves you so much that He gave His life so that you might live forever with Him in heaven. And how can you repay Christ's love? By accepting Him into your heart and by obeying His rul

> Tell me the story of Jesus.
> Write on my heart every word.
> Tell me the story most precious,
> sweetest that ever was heard.
> Fanny Crosby

Big Idea for Parents

Don't Be Embarrassed to Discuss Your Faith: You need not have attended seminary to have worthwhile opinions about your faith. Express those opinions, especially to your children; your kids need to know where you stand.

Today's Prayer

Dear Lord, I am only here on this earth for a while. But, because of Your Son Jesus, I will be with You forever in Heaven. Let me share that Good News with my family and friends.
Amen

Bible Verses
to Remember

Patience is better than strength.

Proverbs 16:32 ICB

Trust the Lord with
all your heart. Don't depend
on your own understanding.
Remember the Lord
in everything you do.
And he will give you success.

Proverbs 3:5-6 ICB

Draw near to God, and He will draw near to you.

James 4:8 Holman CSB

I have come that they may have life, and that they may have it more abundantly.

John 10:10 NKJV

Wisdom begins with respect for the Lord.

Proverbs 9:10 ICB

Do to others what you want them to do to you.

Matthew 7:12 NCV

Now these three remain:
faith, hope, and love.
But the greatest
of these is love.

1 Corinthians 13:13 Holman CSB

Always be humble
and gentle.
Be patient and accept
each other with love.

Ephesians 4:2 ICB

Be still, and know that I am God . . . .

Psalm 46:10 KJV

I am able to do all things through Him who strengthens me.

Philippians 4:13 Holman CSB

The Lord is my shepherd;
I shall not want. He makes me to
lie down in green pastures;
He leads me beside the still waters.
He restores my soul.

Psalm 23:1-3 NKJV

I will give you a new heart and put a new spirit in you . . . .

Ezekiel 36:26 NIV

Do not judge, so that you won't be judged.

Matthew 7:1 Holman CSB

Kind words are like honey—
sweet to the soul and
healthy for the body.

Proverbs 16:24 NLT

If your life honors the name of Jesus, he will honor you.

2 Thessalonians 1:12 MSG

We must not become tired of doing good.

Galatians 6:2 ICB

We love Him because He first loved us.

1 John 4:19 NKJV